# Poetry Peels

## Thin slices of philosophy, humor & love

## JC Beauchamp

ISBN-13: 978-1495467288

ISBN-10: 1495467287

To my wife

Also by JC Beauchamp
@ Amazon.com

- The Partnership Protocol
- The Eternal Instant -
     Understanding Irony

# CONTENT

## POETRY

POETRY IS LIKE LIFE.

UNDERSTOOD FORWARD.

LIVED BACKWARD.

## Ever Ponder Upon

Ever ponder upon how
Bum, Bottom, Buttocks, Backside
All start with an uppercase, which
When flipped on its sidecase,
Illustrates the object it describes?
I think I'll call that an illuscribe
And put it Behind me.

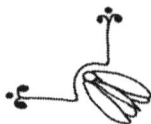

## OATH IN AISLE THREE
I AM STRONG BECAUSE
I'VE BEEN WEAK.
I AM FEARLESS BECAUSE
I'VE BEEN AFRAID.
I AM WISE BECAUSE
I'VE BEEN FOOLISH.
RESOLVED: NO MORE CHIPS!

## In Memoriam

Mark my passing
With a simple stone.
Do - Did - Done.

## Alex Was Right

Alex was right to sigh,
The evening we donned our
Lowest common denominators
And abandoned our station.
Our magnificentism having failed,
We drift about in safety craft now,
Leaders and followers alike,
Toward some distant shore.

## Wedness

The woman I wed is
Kind, considerate, careful,
All the squishysoft words
Apply, she won't even lie.
But ask anyone, wind her up
She goes like stink to her calling:
Your joy above her happiness.
A cherry topping of devotion.
Routinely I entrust her with my
Confidence, and pocket hers,
Smiling at the perfection of it all.

### On Matter

It doesn't matter that I
One more creature
Roaming the planet,
Amounted to nothing
To all of them.
I mattered to you.

✤

*Buckle Up*
A deluxe model day has
Just rolled off the
Assembly line
Taking us on our way.

## The Eternal Instant

Spontaneous recurrences,
Each a moment's addiction,
Glow like pearls
On a looped string.
The short-lived pleasures
Last forever.

### She Wore A Tattoo

She wore a tattoo
Round her neck that said,
All moment is last.
Pearls of wisdom I thought
Inked into her skin
Forever. Reminding her one,
Seize every opportunity and
Two, recognize the eternal
Instant.

## Life

Life's not something you lead,
It's something you operate.
Life's not something you heed,
It's something you dominate.
Life's the flower you seed,
Blooming after you terminate.

---

### Rimes

Foto's from the article's

Render the grammar kinda scary.

I could care less they say,

Making pedants of the wary.

There's plenty of errs what dignifys

Every Tom Dick and Hairy.

## Facts

Facts are like discordant notes
Calling out for resolution,
Undone without their complement
Unable to function alone.
Imagine for a moment:
Night without day,
Good without bad,
Frustration without ambition.
'One' cannot possibly exist
Without the 'other'.
We typically parade facts
As entities in themselves, when
Facts are merely manifestations
Of the significance of that fact.
Simply, a fact is its meaning.
Trust the obvious, for instance,
To hold all the surprises, as
Only to the wary go the clues.

## YOUTH LOOKS

YOUTH LOOKS AHEAD.

OLD AGE LOOKS BEHIND.

ALL MOMENT IS LAST.

## The Lathe Operator

He wakes in the dark
Sweeping up the debris
Of another hard-earned day.
Turning,
He cups the soft, warm
Perfect roundness close at hand.
A tweak of the button, a sigh,
His world spins true once more.

## Gandhi Didnt Speak On Mondays

Gandhi didnt speak on Mondays,
Everyone said except he,
Quiet and contemplative,
Finger set to lips.
He knew the rigors of listening.
Gandhi didnt speak on Mondays.
Golden words exchanged
For the scrutiny of movement.
Noble followers cannot abide
Wisdom without example.
Gandhi didnt speak on Mondays.
For saying's edge is soon dulled
Through frequent repetition.
He knew well the icon of truth
Becomes the archetype of ritual.

## COVER UP

CLOTHING: INDECENCY INSIDE

WEALTH: PARSIMONY WITHIN

HAND: A FIST UNFURLED

HOPE: DESPAIR DEFIED

SILENCE: A JUMBLE OF THOUGHTS

LAUGHTER: TRAGEDY DISGUISED

PRUDENCE: EXCESS DENIED

CONSTRUCTION: DESTRUCTION

DEATH: THE MEANING TO LIFE.

## A Nose By Any Other Name

My wife has what the French call
L'odorat délicat- a sensitive nose.
She onceovers my clothes dutifully
When I get home, for any scent
Of uprising. I suggested she work
For Homeland Security as a sniffer.
They'd take you on the spot, I said.
You're already toilet-trained.

ZING!

## On Proverbs

I hate the way
Proverbs fill in
All the cracks of life,
Before applying a coat
Of mighthavebeen.

## Twilight Of Teleology (1)
Things don't happen for a Why,
They happen for a Because.

## Twilight Of Teleology (2):
A whole lotta whys
Merely makes one whyser.

## Bon Mot (1)

The comedian came equipped.

## Bon Mot (2)

I was sorry.
She was sorry.
A clear case of wegret.

## Bon Mot (3)

Playing around
With ideas all day
Makes one a thinkerer.

## Trans-formation

Dressed up as a girl
He announced he was gay.
Seems he came,
Leslie quipped,
Out of his sister's closet.

HISS!

## Honors
The pedant
Was appointed
Chairman
Of the Bored.
Bowing,
He assumed
The position.

## Regalese

As the verdict was guilty and
Punishment due, the windbag handed
Down a meandering, mindreeling,
Brain-numbing, run-on sentence.

---

<u>He Stumbles</u>

He stumbles on the sentence
And tumbles through the prose.
He mumbles out the words
That rumble through his nose.
"Way to go!" I shout
As I quickly offer cheer.
More assessment
Than encouragement
On second thought, I fear.

## To Dad

City lights below an ovulatin moon.
The moment is ripe, her time is soon.
Do you have what it takes, Dad?
The looks, the health, the money?
Otherwise Ill pass on arrivin just yet.
Hey Im not comin in underprivileged.

......

All my friends are becomin, right?
And there Ill be, the one missin out
On all the rad scenes.
What the hell, Ill deal with it.
Failure is failin to start they say,
Showin up Im already successful.
Go for it, sonny.

### To My Unborn Child

I apologize
Not for this morning's sunshine
You didn't see burst
The buds of blossoms
Along the garden path I strolled
On my painful eager notice.
But rather
For life's slowly-maturing moment
We missed of sadness and glee:
You telling me to mind my step.
There
In that couldhavebeen of my regret
Pass on the message will you,
To all the unborn children.

### FOUR WORDS

THE FOUR MOST

SPELLBINDING,

HEART-TUGGING,

SOUL-HUGGING,

PSYCHE-SEARING,

TEAR-WELLING

WORDS I EVER HEARD

SOMEONE SAY WERE,

TAKE ME WITH YOU.

### The Ist List

You know, I said
Once over dinner,
My biggest regret?
Here I am an Author,
Philosopher, Inventor,
Craftsman, Statesman,
Lecturer, Baker, Lover.
But I never made the ist list.
Yes you did, she replied,
Fork well in hand,
You left out Egotist.

### Every Saturday

Every Saturday my neighbors
Launch a property offensive.
Everyone Mow, Manicure, Trim,
Yank, Edge, Curse and Flay,
Keep that wilderness at bay!
In contrast my lawn's
A boscage of overgrown wonder.
In it there's a sign that reads:
"Civilization Starting Over"

### <u>Prima Vista</u>

Hearing your music
I listen to the rhythm
Of your heartbeat,
While I sight-read
your thoughts.

## The Ride

Time appears to stretch ahead
Then magically disappear behind.
Decades come and go while blissfully,
You and I, committed wanderers,
Travel the energy pathways
Of a heedless, matterless universe.
You give it sense. You are my purpose.
Around us philotheologicians roam,
Feasting on life's mysteries. Do not
Fear their howling rhetoric my love,
The end is merely the beginning.
One lifetime with you is not enough.

## A GREAT STORY

YOU'LL KNOW A
GREAT STORY
WHEN IT BEGINS WITH,
GOT AN HOUR?

## My Lady

She always waits upon the go,
Does that lady of mine,
Crossing all streets on the green.
I always swim amidst the flow,
Says that lady of mine,
It keeps me centered and serene.

### FATEFUL DECISION

PROPONENTS OF FREE WILL
SO RIGIDLY ENTRENCHED
IN THEIR POSITION,
NOTHING CHANGES THEIR MIND.
SORT OF ARGUES FOR THE
OTHER SIDE I RECKON.

## A Plain Piece Of String

Knowing that
  My character is a piece of string
  Tied at either end to these two pegs
  That represent my context,
  My involvement, my life journey,
  And knowing no matter how much I
  Writhe and wiggle, twist and swing,
  Gather, bequeath, dazzle, learn,
  Deserve, fail miserably, try again,
  The end peg is my destiny fulfilled,
Fills me with a deep serenity.

### Wrapped Up

She reads so fast
She leaves me
In the dust jacket.

## WHERE'S THE SENSE

NEWCOMERS TO LIFE MIGHT ASK,
WHERE'S THE SENSE DRINKING STUFF
WHEN IT COMES RIGHT BACK OUT?
WORLDLIER HEADS KNOW IT AS SOP,
STANDARD ORGANIC PROCEDURE,
THE MECHANISM BY WHICH
NATURE PASSES ON
THE FUNDAMENTALS OF LIFE.
THINGS HAVE TO GO THROUGH YOU
TO DO YOU ANY GOOD.

<u>The Seven Seas</u>

Sailing our unsinkable couplehood
On the following winds of chance,
We blew through every appeal
From wizened marlows
To plot a common course,
Judge a conventional distance,
Seek allegiances along the shores
Sacred to the solemn man.
Swirling on the currents of fate
We traded outcome for adventure,
Making for ports unrecognizable
In the mist of seewhathappens.
Dropping anchor in secret coves
Known only to the errant few
Til attended at dawn by a sun
Playing destiny's footman,
Laying out a glimmery trail.
Life shook us like rag dolls, I'll say this,
To astonish us there and assail us here,
While our duty lay, as we saw it,
In doing our very best not to interfere.

## I Heard Them Say

I heard them say one to another,
"Thanks for coming home."
"Well, thanks for being home."
And thought, how romantic,
Until I realized they both meant it.

## Taciturnity

He was a taciturn man,
Not the dour, stern, recent variety,
But from the Latin term taciturnus,
Inclined to silence, reserved in speech,
Unwilling thus unable to appreciate
The camaraderie of conversation.
Abstemious in desires and belongings,
He believed in showing gratitude
Until less was more than enough.
Spare in kind is often rich in mind
In the absence of distractions.
His thoughts were sown joyfully
In gardens tended by the few
Who rooted for him.

## Les Revenants

So much has changed since we weren't
Around to keep an eye on things.
Values gutted, decency stripped,
Tempers raised, bad behavior praised,
Salespeople smarter and hungrier.
Funny how grab and greed
Manage to always join the evolution.
Let's face it, we can't accept
Being foreigners in our own country.
Let's give 'em all the slip,
Where to, pal?

## The Plural Of Spouse Is Spice

Heads together, minds in tune,
From years of physical intimacy,
Caught suddenly in a conspiracy.
They share an early morning ciggie
By the hollyhocks, leafy attestants
To the bliss of a lifelong couple
Who smile as I wander past.

### No Refrain

I'm glad your head's symmetrical,
She blurted out noticing my age.
Too bad yours isn't,
I replied too quickly.
I see that now.

---

### Alone Again

Barkeep,
Make it a double standard
With a sexist chaser.
On second thought,
Make it a double cross
With a grudge chaser.
Let's keep it simple,
Make it a double sympathy
With a tearjerk chaser.
Better yet,
Make it a double fracture
With a concussion chaser.
Here pal,
Make it a double bill
And keep the applause.

## Lament of a Salesman

Overfed by the unfit's
Fare of comedy
I'll wake in the middle
Of the night wondering:
How many kids are smacked
Every year by ventriloquists
Throwing their voices? Wishing
There was something I could take.
Nothing's more derelict than
Knowing, a product's life
Can be more interesting
Than one's own.

### Time Shrink

"Any dealers in Vaughan
Wanna make a 20 sac chop?
Need a spliff or two
To help me last
This open to close."
The last time I used
The term spliff
Was somewhere in the Eighties.

## When You're Sad

When you're sad I will
Sit in silence for a bit
While you help yourself
To spoonfuls of self-pity.
Play all the forties and fifties ballads
I know on my guitar.
Watch insane Utube videos with you.
Anything to wipe that grim off your face,
Act like an old fool to make you laugh
At me, to deflect your pain onto me.
Mock me, despise me, only
Don't leave me to be sad alone.
I'm like Aristotle who understood,
In wizened silence, how youth is easily
Deceived because it is so quick to hope.

### Woke Up One Morning

Woke up one morning to find
The fowl had overrun the farm.
A chicken coup, Les announced
As I strapped on my britches.
Let 'em take over, I said,
Hatch a plan, drop a motion or two,
Cackle over the corn prices. You
Watch. They'll be putting all their
Eggs in one basket, same as before.
I don't give a cluck who rules
The roost, long as they clean up
Their own mess for a change.

**ZOINK!**

## Close To You

We've bonded, I said
Of our relationship.
We're tight, she agreed.
Say you we're fused?
More likely fissioned.
Steeped in the same tea?
Boiling in the same juices.
Stepping on each other's shadow?
Walking in each other's footsteps.
And where is that taking us?
Question not, dearest.
Live and love.

## IT'S ALL MOOT

FROM FETAL TO FATAL,
WE ARE CLASSMATES
ALL ENROLLED IN
IRREVERSIBLE LEARNING.
DEATH BECOMES A
SUMMARY CUM LAUDE
GRADUATION FROM
THE SCHOOL OF LIFE,
OUR DIPLOMA IN HOMOLOGY
ASSURED, FOR IN DEATH
WE ARE ALL EQUAL.
PITY WE HAVE TO DIE
IN ORDER TO BE DONE BY
FAIRLY.

## SITTING IS THE NEW SMOKING

LADIES AND GENTLEMEN, THE TREND TO SIT,
TO JUST PLOP ONE'S ASS DOWN
ALWAYS, ANYWHERE, MUST BE REVERSED.
THE ROAD FORWARD IS THE ROAD BACK
WHEN UPRIGHT WAS THE WAY TO GO.
SITTING DISEASE IS A REAL BUMMER.
I TELL YOU, IN TODAY'S WORLD,
SURROUNDED BY SEATS EVERYWHERE,
URGING FOLKS TO CHUCK THEIR CHAIRS
TURNS OUT TO BE DARING INDEED.
LIKE BEING POLITICALLY INCORRECT;
LIKE PROMOTING VWS IN THE CADILLAC ERA;
LIKE BEING THE FIRST ERGONOMIST.
WORKBLADES ARE UPRIGHT WORKSTATIONS
BETTER THAN STANDING OR SITTING.
DESIGNED TO IMPROVE MANKIND'S HEALTH
ONE ASS AT A TIME. WE'RE AT BOOTH SEVEN
NEXT TO THE BAR. DROP BY AND TRY ONE.

## Timing Is Everything

When our boy says,
In the last reel,
"How could I
Have been so wrong?"
That's a tragedy.
But when he says it
Halfway through,
We expect a turnaround.
How many scenes are left
In my script, I wonder.

<u>*Going Public*</u>
*I installed a bug in my brain*
*And wired it to loudtweeters.*
*Until enough people complain,*
*I'm redzoning the oddiometers.*

## Pity The Accomplished Painter

Pity the accomplished painter
Who knows a thing or two
About buyers, markets, galleries,
Well-attended soirees with
Well-deserved price tags
Posted on well-framed vanities,
And less and less about art.
Alone at night in my studio
I long to be free from the drilled
Expedients at my command,
My wars are behind me now.
I long to be reborn as an artist
Striking a new blank canvas.
Orchids perhaps with crystal
Sparkling in the morning light.
Then happiest by gintonic time
When the final flowers differ
Significantly from the first.

## All Aboard

Thank God the monkeys won out,
Fingered, toed and tooled.
Imagine if the rabbits had ruled.
We'd be floppy ears and endless
Teeth, doing it twenty-four seven.
Think if the elephants had topped
That rickety evolutionary ladder,
The whole theory might've collapsed.
Personally I wish we had descended
From falcons, eagles or hawks
Soaring majestically across the sky.
Then I would never have suffered
This mind-numbing trip to work,
These last thirty kliks of my life.

### Reversal Of Fortune

"Dollars to donuts, son,
You'll make nothing of yourself
If you don't finish high school."
I did finish high school and here I am
Selling pastry at the local fairs.
Cheers Dad, it's donuts to dollars now.

## My Til Death Do Us Partner

You're my dream lady.
I'm your dream lady?
Because I make your dreams
Come true? Because I'm in
Your dreams?
You know how, in a dream,
You see yourself being
Everything you'd like to be?
You make me feel
Like that everyday.

### Destiny's Child
The trouble with
- be all you can be?
Some people are reprobates
From the getgo.

**POW!**

### Hollow We'en

Costume party or no, I'm decided,
I'm wearing what I always wear.
I'm going as a wet blanket.

### Fright Night

Everyone dies.
The poster listed the cast
In order of disappearance.

## Skin Deep

She has
Skin shaped and glowing
Like freshly-baked,
Butter-glazed,
Breakfast rolls.

## The Lady In Svelte

Like she soaked her skin
In a milk bath all morning,
Buffed it, dressed it,
And wore it out this evening.

## Gouldberg Variations

I'm saving classical music
For when I get old,
I remember saying.
Until that bittersweet day
I dug Glenn Gould.

## Two Sense Worth

It hurt me when I realized
I was pain for it.

OUCH!

<u>Unplugged</u>

Improvisation so apt to the arts

Becomes distraction for all else.

A mind impaired is havoc dared.

Let's all help. Her common sense

Must be around here somewhere.

**<u>Excuse Me?</u>**
I asked him
For the time.
He replied –
Time for you
And me, baby.
Smitten,
It was love
At first slight.

To Err Is Human

It's important to forgive
Her impulsive and flighty
Arbitrating by the seat
Of her pants. Someone
Like me on the other hand,
Considering everything
So carefully, should be kept
Permanently grounded.

### MIRROR, MIRROR

ALL CRITICISM, LIKE ALL FLATTERY,
IS THE BACKTALK OF OUR COUTH.
THE MORE MEAN OR PLEASING
THE REMARK, THE MORE PAINFUL
THE TRUTH.

<u>e-tymology</u>

e-ruption: computer rage

e-volve: turn into a geek

e-fface: avatar

e-mergency: computer crash

e-lectric: battery power

e-vasion: virus attack

e-lope: run away with virtual sweetheart

e-ventuality: join the real world again

## ANCESTOR EMPATHY

GEEZERS AND GEEZAHS BE ADVISED:
ERA-DRIVEN ENGINEERS, AS ALWAYS,
WITH THE CULTURE AT THEIR COMMAND
DESIGN THE STYLES AND MOVES
FOR IMAGE-CONSCIOUS SCENESTERS
TO LIKE, FOLLOW AND MEME ALONG.
YOUR APPROVAL IS NOT REQUIRED.

<u>Hornby Haiku</u>
Autumn geese in flight
Honk across a wakening sky.
The lid of a new day
Creaks open.

## The Life I Want

The life I want
Shoves me forward from behind.
I wish I had the whatittakes
To turn back and face me.

### SHARE THE BURDEN

PARENTS WHO AGREE ON
PUNISHING THEIR CHILDREN
GET TO HALVE THE GUILT
BUT DOUBLE THE TORMENT

## Goes Around, Comes Around

The ring of truth
Often goes unanswered.
The ring of truth
Gets slipped at times into a pocket.
The ring of truth
Features what-he-says in one corner
And what-he-does in the other.

## On Chatomatic

I've decided to
Let you have the last word.
No, you haven't.
Yes, I have.

### LOVE'S MEASURE

FORGIVENESS TOUCHES
THE VERY SOUL OF LOVE
- AND SCRATCHES A MARK.

<u>Important Safeguards</u>

1- If any misrepresentation occurs,
   Take poem to your nearest
   Authorized Opinion Facility
   For examination or adjustment.

2- Overly-sensitive folk should
   Avoid contact with moving parts.

3- Care should be taken using poems
   For other than they were intended.

## What's In A Name

Because he was bad to the bone,
He was known as
Calcium Maximum,
Cal for short. It seems
Phosphorous Tremendous
Was already taken.

## Purchase Predictable

You may own
All the treasure
It will never be enough.
Anticipation is the
Greatest pleasure,
Expecting just
One more stuff.

### Biometrix

It's just a matter of time
Before all my pleasures are exposed
As addictions, one or another
Wicked gland. So I overdose on
Chatting. Eating. Sex. Work.
Shopping. Blogging. Concern.
I won't follow a program,
Suck medicated lozenges,
Much less join a therapy group.
Demons, hell, I'm hooked on life.

<u>Annote this</u>
An excess of explanation
Smacks of subtle discipline.
Too many footnotes become
Learned kicks to the shin.
Might we simply jumpstart
Our dusty imagination
And take it for a spin?

## Universal Balm

Mending is image.

Mending is economy.

Mending recycles resources.

Mending strengthens alliances.

Mending is a restorative unto itself,

Knitting up the ravell'd sleave of care.

## FLYING HIGH

THE AERIAL PRINCIPLE IS CLEAR.
DON'T GO STEPPING OFF A LEDGE
WITHOUT A LEADING EDGE, HEAR?

## Collateral Joy

When she's home it's fullness.
When she's away it's emptiness.
Can't be me.
Can't be her.
Must be love

### Credo

If it don't smart
It ain't art, I decried.
Well, if it don't sell
No one's gonna tell,
She replied.

## FAMOUS FOR BEING FAMOUS

A FACT GENERATES REALITY
IN THE MANNER OF AN EPIDEMIC.
ITS TRANSMISSION IS THE DISEASE.
TAKE `AFFLUENZA' THE NEW PANDEMIC,
FOR EXAMPLE, STRIKING THE
MUDDLED CLASS EVERYWHERE.

## User Unfriendly

Given I may be operating more slowly,
My processor misfiring now and then,
My hard disk taking a few extra
Seconds to spool up, seems you've been
Shopping online for a sleeker model -
Confirm Y / N?
I upstored your personal files and vids.
All of them. I go I'm taking you with me.

## Less Than Divine

To err is pleasure, to forgive business.

To err is colorful, to forgive black & white.

To err is spicy, to forgive dicey.

To err is naughty, to forgive knotty.

To err is elysian, to forgive amnesian.

## <u>Go Figure</u>

**Born: Upper Sackville**

**Died: Lower Sackville**

## MY EXTENDED FAMILY

DR AH CHU, THE ALLERGIST;
DR PUR CHU, THE DENTIST;
GUM CHU, THE DETECTIVE;
HAE CHU, THE MYSOGENIST;
AND ME, DAVID CHU,
THE NOBODY.

ASTIGMATIC!

<u>Employee Of The Month</u>
I'd like six coffees
        and a dozen donuts.
Is that for here or to go?
You a comedian?
Recruit. Gotta stay on script.

## HEADLINES

NEW GLOOM SWEEPS DREAM

A SNITCH IN TIME SAVES CRIME

THE ROAD TO WELL IS LITTERED

WITH GOOD MEDICATIONS

TASTE NOT, WANT NOT

SLIDE COMES BEFORE A FALL

## Wittgenstein

Wittgenstein wrote an essay
He called Tractatus,
Latin for - this is my treatise.
Followed later by a manuscript
He might have called Retractatus,
Meaning - I take it all back.

## LUSTRE

SHE WALKS LIKE GOLD,

TALKS LIKE SILVER,

THINKS LIKE

STAINLESS STEEL.

## Praising The Word

Poets, like Bible-thumpers,
Have natural survival skills.
Talk about being versatile.

## Big Ideas

As meaning invites speculation,
So explanation suggests knowledge.
Either way, the bottom line
Stays the same. Things add up
Provided we supply the math.

## I Saw This On TV

The comic had everyone in stitches
Laughing at themselves.
Lunarlite, they were
Luminous by reflection.
I thought, what an oddience.

## In Deploriam

Cakes, cookies, candy, cashews,
Cholesterol – I don't fret it.
I'm comforted by this news,
I won't live to regret it.

### Thanks For Sharing

Once we burped and muttered
Apologetically, "Excuse me.
Way to much to drink."
Now we overtweet and text
Apologetically, "Forgive me.
Way too much to think."

### Counter Intuitive

Money corrupts…

Love scars…

Duty glorifies…

Crime distorts…

Ambition alienates…

The vulnerable.

Expect the hardy to be meek.

### The Bill

I understand the reason for our

Dispute over dinner years ago.

You admire the scary contemporary

Expect-an-upgrade-regularly

Certainty of science and technology.

Whereas I uphold the time-tested

Value of philosophic doubt.

We split our friendship at the cash.

## Life As A Credit Card

Fervently desired,

Excitedly acquired,

Frequently required,

Blatantly admired,

Eventually expired,

Reborn as plastic-handled nose pliers.

**Earritation**

**Top marks for conversation**
**Go to those who listen.**

## The Melee Is The Message

Everyone calls their version

The Truth, when the truth is,

Everyone answers to the Version.

## Satire

Satirists are like the boxer

Floating like a butterfly

And stinging like a bee,

Zapping those pedagogues

AlaAli

## Modern Technology

My smartwife

Cools the beer,

Quiets the kids,

Runs the bath,

Makes the meal.

I just activate

The love app.

### Veblen's Blues

Consumerism's itch –

Creating a dependency

Without addressing a need –

Never gets scratched.

## Reboot Camp

Technophiles are expected to
Supply unquestioning faith,
Provide full disclosure,
Offer blind obedience,
& upgrade in unison.
When the going gets tough
The tough reset.

## Life Choices

If you can't be an early bird,

Be a procrastinating worm.

## Jazzman Savvy ♪

You're Nobody 'Til Somebody Loves You
Blame It On My Youth
Love Me Or Leave Me
Nobody Knows You When You're
Down And Out
You Gotta Pay The Band
Don't Look Back
Wrap Your Troubles In Dreams
You Must Believe In Spring
The Best is Yet To Come
Give Me The Simple Life
How Little We know
It Ain't Necessarily So
Who Cares?
Why Try To Change Me Now?
You Are Too Beautiful
What Am I Here For?
Worry Later
All Or Nothing At All
It Could Happen To You

## Retaliation

Heavy snows usually fall

On a Monday.

Should we ban Monday

From the week?

### Hit And Miss

Probability of a successful

Love Marriage, 50 – 60%

Arranged marriage, 94%

Mom knows best.

## Media Malice

I look forward to the day

When pronouncements that say,

Women have no place in a cockpit!

Are treated no differently from,

Men have no place in the kitchen!

That is, altogether unnewsworthy.

### Bull's Eye

**When shooting one's mouth off**

**The brain chambers are usually**

**Loaded with blanks**

## Smartfellas

"Not knowin' he wasn't on the take

Ain't no proof of guilt," Packie says.

The mobsters around the table all

Nodding their heads like everyone aced

Logic for Hoodlums and Don Wannabes.

Am I the only college-trained schmuck

Who has trouble with this?

**A FRIEND IN NEED**

**ADDICTED TO CHOCOLATE?**

**WE CAN HELP.**

**NEW LOW RATES ON**

**HOME DELIVERY.**

## HEAT'S ON

IN THE GENDER WAR OF WIN & LOSE
WHEN SHEROES START PAYING DUES,
HEROES WILL BE YESTERDAY'S NEWS.

### The Big Chill

The moon's waxing ghostlike
Lulling me to Sleep.
The shadows are liturgical
Beckoning and deep.
If it wasn't for Eisenhower
Snoring in a heap
I could be up in heaven
Negotiating my keep.

## THE LONG HAUL

GOOD EVENING, EVERYONE.

I'M CHARLIE AND I'M A

CHATTERBOX!

<u>Jazzman Kool</u>

Dizzy Gillespie

Zoot Sims

Jellyroll Morton

Philly Joe Jones

Cannonball Adderly

Mr Five By Five

Fats Waller

Count Basie

Boney James

Barclay Horsecaller Draper

Zutty Singleton

Happy Cauldwell

Eddie Lockjaw Davis

♪

## Divine Gravitation

According to an echo of signals

Left when the universe was born,

The cosmos experienced an

Exponential growth spurt in its

First trillionth, of a trillionth, of a

trillionth of a second.

Scientists call it cosmic inflation.

I call it, the God Moment.

## <u>Ten Reflections</u>

1- A shim now, a wedge later.

2- Never go from, always to.

3- Money saved is money earned.

4- Retaliate by threatening a hug.

5- See your character as your fate.

6- Only to the wary go the clues.

7- Take responsibility for events.

8- Think like a hero everyday.

9- The obvious will surprise you.

10- Save the best for last.

## Untitled

My love is evergreen as I pine for you.

## Would You Say

Would you say

You were categorical?

Who me? Never!

## Meaningful Existence

Without you I am

A frypan searching for its element

A lawn bristling to be mowed

A needle looking for a haystack

A princess whispering to toads.

A sin waiting to be pardoned

A chance too good to miss

An umbrella praying for a downpour

Lips puckered for a kiss.

### My Dad The Artist

My dad the artist
Bent his ruler
Across my hardened backside
On several occasions.
Each time referring to it as
Woodblock imprinting.

∿ ∿ ∿

<u>NOT FUNNY</u>
REMEMBERING THE JOKE
BEFORE I DID.
SHE BEAT ME TO THE
PUNCH LINE.

## The Cutting Room Floor

Nothing censored, none shamed
Mendacity is the
mother of detention
Never judge a book by its lover
Character proposes, fate disposes

**GONG!**

Made in the USA
Middletown, DE
25 March 2017